The Immortal Life of Henrietta Lacks

by Rebecca Skloot

Study Guide

Pembroke Notes

First published by Dog Ear Publishing
4010 W. 86th Street, Ste H
Indianapolis, IN 46268
www.dogearpublishing.net

ISBN: 978-1-4575-2414-1

This book is printed on acid-free paper.

Printed in the United States of America

PEMBROKE NOTES

Common Core and Alaska State Standards

Reading Informational Text

1. Cite strong and thorough textural evidence to support analysis of what the text says explicitly as well as implicit inferences drawn from the text.

2. Determine a central idea of a text and analyze its development over the course of the text, including how it emerges and is shaped and refined by specific details: restate and summarize main ideas or events, in correct sequence when necessary, after reading the text.

3. Analyze in detail how an author's ideas or claims are developed and refined by particular sentences, paragraphs, or larger portions of a text.

4. Determine an author's point of view on purpose in a text and analyze how an author uses rhetoric to advance that point of view or purpose.

5. Delineate and evaluate the argument and specific claims in a text.

Writing Standards

1. Write informative/explanatory texts to examine and convey complex ideas, concepts, and information clearly and accurately

through the effective selection, organization, and analysis of content.

2. Produce clear and coherent writing in which the development, organization, style, and features are appropriate to task, genre, purpose, and audience.

3. Use technology, including the Internet, to produce, publish, and update individual or shared writing products, taking advantage of technology's capacity to line to other information to display information flexibly and dynamically.

4. Draw evidence from literary or informational texts to support analysis reflection, and research.

5. Write routinely over extended time frames (time for research, reflection, and revision) and shorter time frames (a single sitting a day or two) for a range of tasks, and issues, building on others' ideas and expressing their own clearly and persuasively.

Language Standards

1. Demonstrate command of the conventions of Standard English, capitalization, punctuation, and spelling when writing.

2. Apply knowledge of language of language to understand how language functions in different contexts, to make effective choices for meaning or style, and comprehend more fully when reading or listening.

3. Determine or clarify the meaning of unknown and multiple-meaning words and phrases based on grades 9-12 reading and content, choosing flexibly from a range of strategies.

A FEW WORDS ABOUT THIS BOOK

Q. Why did the author, Rebecca Skloot decide to write in dialect exactly as written?

A. "If you pretty up how people spoke and change the things they said, that's dishonest."

Q. Since Henrietta Lacks died many years ago, how did the author research this topic?

A. She relied on interviews, legal documents, and medical records to recreate scenes from Henrietta's life.

Q. What issues does the history of Henrietta Lacks raise?

A. Issues raised include science, ethics, race, and class.

Prologue: The Woman in the Photograph

Predict why a caption beneath of photo of the woman on the cover is "Henrietta Lacks, Helen Lane or Helen Larson."

Q. How extensively are Henrietta's cells used?

A. Her cells traveled in space missions and have helped in medical advances such as polio vaccine, chemotherapy, cloning, gene mapping and in vitro fertilization.

Q. Where did the author first develop an interest in cells?

A. After transferring to an alternative school, Donald Defler intro-duced words like *mitosis* and *kinase inhibitors* to a junior- college class that offered high -school credit.

Q. Why are cells amazing things?

A. There are about one trillion of them in our bodies and it would take thousands of them to fit on the tip of a pen. They make up all our tissues, which in turn make up our organs.

Q. The genome performs what duties?

A. The genome tells cells when to grow and divide and make sure the cells do their jobs like controlling heartbeats or helping brains understand things.

Q. What is the purpose of mitosis?

A. Cell division makes it possible for embryos to grow into babies, and for our bodies to create new cells for healing wounds or replenishing blood we've lost.

Q. What happens when something impedes this fine-tuned machine?

A. Just one enzyme misfiring, or one wrong protein activation, and you could have cancer. Mitosis goes haywire and the cancer spreads.

Q. Why were Henrietta's cells different from other cells?

A. They reproduced an entire generation every twenty-four hours, and they never stopped. They became the first immortal human cells ever grown in a laboratory.

Q. Henrietta's cell participated in what research?

A. Henrietta's cells were used for research in cancer, herpes, leukemia, influenza, hemophilia, and Parkinson's disease; also lactose digestion, STDs, appendicitis, human longevity, and mosquito mating.

Q.   Henrietta's cells have become the standard laboratory
     _____.

Q.   Her cells were **omnipresent.** What does omnipresent mean?

A.   **Omnipresent** means present at all times in all places.

Q.   What did Jet mean when it said the "family was angry"?

A.   They were angry because Henrietta's cells were being sold for $25 a vial, and angry that articles had been published about the cells without their knowledge.

Q.   How important was the first phone call to the author?

A.   It was the beginning of a decade long adventure through scientific laboratories, hospitals, and mental institutions while visiting Nobel laureates, grocery store clerks, convicted felons, and a professional con artist.

Q.   What was the importance of Deborah's story to Rebecca Skloot?

A.   Because of Deborah's strength and resilience the two women became part of each other's story.

Q.   Explain the difference in the cultures of Rebecca and Deborah?

A.   Rebecca grew up white and agnostic in the Pacific Northwest, half New York Jew and half Midwestern Protestant. Deborah was a deeply religious black Christian from the South.

Q.   What is "woo-woo stuff?

A.   "Woo-woo stuff" is all things supernatural.

Q.   How did Rebecca grow through her research of the Lack's family?

A.   She says, "The Lackses challenged everything I thought I knew about faith, science, journalism, and race."

Q.   Explain the irony in "Deborah's Voice."

A.   "If my mother done so much for medicine, how come her family can't afford to see no doctors?"

CHAPTER 1

The Exam

1. What was the condition of racism in 1951 when David Lacks took his wife to John Hopkins Hospital?

    A. Answers will vary. Possible answers include dialogue about **the Civil Rights Movement.**

        A growing group of Americans spoke out against inequality and injustice during the 1950s. African Americans had been fighting against racial discrimination for centuries; during the 1950s, however, the struggle against racism and segregation entered the mainstream of American life. For example, in 1954, in the landmark Brown v. Board of Education case, the Supreme Court declared that "separate educational facilities" for black children were "inherently unequal." This ruling was the first nail in Jim Crow's coffin.

        Many Southern whites resisted the Brown ruling. They withdrew their children from public schools and enrolled them in all-white "segregation academies," and they used violence and intimidation to prevent blacks from asserting their rights. In 1956, more than 100 Southern congressmen even signed a "Southern Manifesto" declaring that they would do all they could to defend segregation.

        Despite these efforts, a new movement was born. In December 1955, a Montgomery activist named was arrested for refusing to give her seat on a city bus to a white person. Her arrest sparked a 13-month boycott of the city's buses by its black citizens, which only ended when the bus companies stopped discriminating against African American passengers. Acts of "nonviolent resistance" like the boycott helped shape the of the next decade.

Henrietta was only allowed to use the "colored" bathroom.

Additional links: www.loc.gov/rr/program/bib/civilrights/external.html

2. What were the first symptoms of Henrietta's disease?

    A. "I got a knot inside me."

3. Why did Henrietta keep the symptoms from her doctor?

    A. She was afraid a doctor would take her womb and make her stop having children.

4. Where was Henrietta directed when she tested negative for syphilis?

    A. She was directed to John Hopkins gynecology clinic.

5. How did the era of Jim Crow figure into the care Henrietta received at John Hopkins?

    A. Staff was likely to send black patients away, even if it meant they might die in the parking lot. Even Hopkins, which did treat black patients, segregated them in colored wards, and had colored-only fountains.

        Additional links: www.ferris.edu/jimcrow/links/misclink/examples

6. All doctors keep personal charts of their patients. After reading Henrietta's chart, what value do these charts give the doctors?

    A. Charts give a quick sketch of their patients' lives and related or unrelated medical conditions.

7. Why was walking into Hopkins like entering a foreign country for Henrietta?

   A. She didn't "speak the language." She did not read or write much and she had not studied science in school.

CHAPTER 2

Clover

1. Why did her grandfather, Tommy Lacks, raise Henrietta?

    A. When Henrietta's mother died in childbirth, her father, Johnny Pleasant, knowing he could not raise their 10 children, divided them up among relatives.

2. Describe the "home-house."

    A. The "home-house" was a former slave quarters, a four-room log cabin, and plank floors, gas lanterns where water was hauled from a creek nearby.

3. How did Henrietta spend the rest of her life with David (Day) Lacks?

    A. First they were cousins growing up in their grandfather's home, and then they were husband and wife.

4. How was life growing up in Clover from 1920-1942?

    A. They tended to animals and gardens and worked in the tobacco fields. They did not finish school. They spent summer at swimming holes and with bonfires playing games and trips to South Boston during harvest season. Clover was a dusty old Main Street filled with Model As around a movie theater, bank, jewelry store, doctor's office, hardware store, and several churches.

5. When visiting the movie theater's black section, they sat next to the projector that clicked like a **metronome.** What is a metronome?

   A. A metronome is an instrument designed to mark exact time by a regularly repeated tick.

6. Who was Crazy Joe?

   A. Crazy Joe was another cousin who was in love with Henrietta.

7. Henrietta and Day had son Lawrence and a daughter Elsie, who was "just simple". What did this mean?

   A. Years later, people would use terms like epilepsy, mental retardation, or neurosyphilis to Elsie's condition.

8. What was Turner Station?

   A. Turner Station was a small black community next to the Bethlehem Steel's Sparrows Point steel mill.

9. Why did it seem the Turner Station had won the lottery?

   A. After Pearl Harbor attack, the demand for steel skyrocketed producing concrete-reinforcing bars. Barbed wire, nails and steel for cars, refrigerators, and military ships.

10. How did Henrietta and Day become part of the "Great Migration" to the "Promised Land?"

    A. Cousin Fred bought Day a bus ticket to Turner Station, soon followed by Henrietta and the kids.

    Additional links: www.louisdiggs.com/meadow/home.html

CHAPTER 3

Diagnosis and Treatment

1. What was the initial diagnosis after biopsy?

    A. Epidermoid carcinoma of the cervix, Stage I. Most cervical cancers are carcinomas, which grow from the epithelial cells that cover the cervix and protect its surface.

2. What are the two types of cervical carcinomas?

    A. Invasive carcinomas, which have penetrated the surface of the cervix, and noninvasive carcinomas, "sugar-icing carcinoma" which have not.

        Additional links: www.cdc.gov/cancer/cervical/links.htm

3. What is *carcinoma in situ?*

    A. TelLind believe carcinoma in situ was the early stage of invasive carcinoma, now diagnosed through the Pap smear developed by George Papanicolaou, a Greek researcher.

4. What is Pap smear?

    A. A test developed by George Papanicolaou involving scraping cells from the cervix.

5. What stood in the way of seeing a 70 percent decrease in cervical cancer?

    A. Many women, like Henrietta, did not get the test, and few doctors knew how to interpret the results because he did not know how the various stages looked under the microscope.

6. What were TeLinde's goals?

    A. He wanted to minimize "unjustifiable hysterectomies" by documenting what wasn't cervical cancer and urging surgeons to verify smear results with biopsies before operating. He also wanted women with carcinoma in situ to get aggressive treatment.

7. How did TeLinde and other scientists conduct research?

    A. They felt since patients were being treated for free in public wards, it was fair to use them as research in lieu of payment.

8. Why did TeLinde call George Gey?

    A. TeLinde believed if he could find a way to grow living samples from normal cervical tissue and both types of cancerous tissue, he could compare all three. He could prove he was right all along. George Gey had spent three decades trying to grow malignant cells outside the body.

9. Why did he call himself "the world's most famous vulture, feeding on human specimens almost constantly?"

    A. He took cells wherever he could get them.

10. What was the treatment for Henrietta's cervical cancer?

    A. Henrietta signed an operation permit then her invasive cancer was treated with radium through Brack plaques.

        Additional links: www.cancer.org/cancer/cervicalcancer/detailedguide/cervical-cancer-treating-radiation

11. How does radium work?

    A. Radium destroys any cells it encounters, including cells.

    Additional links: www.orau.org/ptp/collection/brachytherapy/misc.htm

12. What also occurred during surgery?

    A. Dr. Lawrence Wharton, without Henrietta's permission, shaved two dime-sized pieces of tissue from her cervix.

13. Why did scientists at the lab consider Henrietta's lab samples as tedious?

    A. They were sure Henrietta's cells would die just like all the others.

CHAPTER 4

The Birth of HeLa

1. What were the obstacles to growing cells successfully?

    A. No one knew exactly what nutrients they needed to supply or how best to supply them.

2. Why were these nutrients called witches' brews?

    A. Recipes includes plasma of chickens, puree of calf fetuses, special salts, and blood from human umbilical cords.

3. How did Gey obtain chicken blood?

    A. Gey would grab a screaming chicken by the legs, yank it upside down from its cage, and wrestle it to its back on a butcher block. He'd hold its feet in one hand and pin its neck motionless to the wood with his elbow. He then would swab the bird's chest with alcohol, and plunge a syringe needle into the chicken's heart to draw blood.

        Additional links: http://users.rcn.com/jkimball.ma.ultranet/BiologyPages/C/CancerCellsInCulture.html

4. What was the biggest problem facing cell culture?

    A. Contamination

5. What was the importance of Gold Dust Twins soap?

    A. Minnie, a local woman hired my Margaret Gey, washed the
        laboratory using only Gold Dust Twins soap. Margaret
        bought a boxcar full of it when it was thought the company
        was going out of business.

6. How did Margaret make a case of sterility?

    A. Mary could be found with a clean white gown, surgical cap
        and mask, and then walked to her cubicle, one of four air-
        tight rooms George had built by hand in the center of the
        room. Hot steam killed anything that might damage the
        cells. She then hosed the cubicle's cement floor with water
        and scoured her workbench with alcohol. Once inside the
        sterilized cubicle she lit a Bunsen burner and used its flame
        to sterilize test tubes and used scalpel blades.

        Additional   links: http://www.protocolonline.org/prot/
        General_Laboratory_Techniques/Sterile_Technique

7. The author portrays George Gey as a reckless visionary. What
    supports that statement?

    A. He was spontaneous, quick to start dozens of projects at
        once, filling the lab and his basement at home with half-built
        machines, partial discoveries, and piles of junkyard scraps
        only he could imagine using in a lab.

8. What was his most important invention?

    A. He created a roller-tube culturing technique, which included
        a roller drum (called a whirligig), a cylinder with holes for
        special test tubes called roller tubes.

9. What simile described the rapid growth of Henrietta's cells?

    A. Spreading like crabgrass.

CHAPTER 5

"Blackness Be Spreadin All Inside"

1. Henrietta was a fun-loving woman. What information supports that statement?

    A. Various answers including Sadie's quote, "Hennie made life come alive—bein with her was like bein with fun."

2. What behaviors of Elsie's led Henrietta and Day to take her to the Crownsville State Hospital—formerly known as the Hospital for the Negro Insane?

    A. She ran into walls and doors, burned herself against the woodstove, grabbing the family mule by the tale.

3. Henrietta's children acted differently when she was not around. What evidence supports that statement?

    A. Various answers including Lawrence running off to the pier.

4. Why was it necessary for Henrietta to tell her cousins, Margaret and Sadie, she was sick?

    A. She needed their help.

5. Why did the doctors tattoo two black dots on Henrietta's abdomen?

    A. They were targets so he could aim the radiation into the same area each day, but rotate between spots to avoid burning her skin too much in one place.

6. One of the side effects of radium treatment was infertility. Why was this upsetting for Henrietta?

    A. Although warning patients about this side effect was standard practice, Henrietta was not informed of this and by the time she found out it was too late.

7. How had the treatment left her skin?

    A. The skin from her breasts to her pelvis were charred a deep black from the radiation.

CHAPTER 6

"Lady's on the Phone"

1. What did Roland Pattillo mean when he told Rebecca in 1999, "Oh child, you have no idea what you're getting into?"

    A. They (the family) won't talk to you.

2. Why was Pattillo grilling Rebecca about her intentions as an author?

    A. He did not trust her sincerity.

3. What was the Tuskegee syphilis study?

    A. Researchers watched hundreds of African-American men with syphilis die an agonizing death even after a cure had been found.

    Additional links: www.cdc.gov/tuskegee/timeline.htm

    http://www.infoplease.com/spot/bhmtuskegee1.html

    http://www.npr.org/programs/morning/features/2002/jul/tuskegee/

4. News "spread like pox" describes refers to?

    A. How quickly rumors can travel.

5.   What were the Mississippi Appendectomies?

    A.   These were unnecessary hysterectomies performed on poor black women to stop them from reproducing, and to give young doctors a chance to practice the procedure.

    Additional links: http://www.curethis.org/showDiary.do?diaryId=105

    http://mississippiappendectomy.wordpress.com

6,   What is Sickle-cell anemia?

    A.   It is a disease that affects blacks almost exclusively.

    Additional links: http://www.seattlecca.org/diseases/sickle-cell-disease-overview.cfm?gclid=CNSkg4XkorgCFYaDQ-godvB4AVg

7.   Why did Pattillo finally say to Rebecca, "Do have patience. You'll need that more than anything."

    A.   Deborah, Henrietta's only living daughter almost had a stroke dealing with all the inquiries regarding her mother's cells and her death.

8.   Rebecca's initial contact with Deborah was not what she expected. Why?

    A.   She began talking right away and did not want to stop.

9.   Any further interviews would have to wait. Why?

    A.   Deborah said, "Only thing to do is convince the men."

10.   How did a young boy know why Rebecca was calling?

    A.   The only time white people called Day was when they wanted something having to do with HeLa cells.

CHAPTER 7

The Death and Life of Cell Culture

1. What was behind the quick distribution of cells to other scientists?

    A. By sending cells to anyone who wanted them, Gey hoped that "we will be able to learn a way by which cancer cells can be damaged or completely wiped out."

2. Gey refereed to these cells as his _____.

    A. "precious babies"

3. By 1951, cell culture had become less a medical procedure than something out of a scary science-fiction movie. Why was this reference made?

    A. Alexis Carrel grew his "immortal chicken heart."

    Additional links: http://www.bluesci.org/?p=3283

    http://embryo.asu.edu/pages/alexis-carrels-immortal-chick-heart-tissue-cultures-1912-1946

4. Why would Carrel praise Hitler?

    A. He was a eugenicist that believed organ transplantation and life extension were ways to preserve the superior white race which he believed was being polluted by less intelligent and inferior stock, namely the poor, uneducated, and nonwhite. Hitler took "energetic measures" in this direction.

Additional links: http://www.eugenicsarchive.org/eugenics/

5.   What was the frenzy about his work?

    A.   He believed that light could kill cell cultures, so techs worked in his lab covered in long black robes, heads covered in black hoods with small slits cut out for their eyes. He wanted to fix the part in the Constitution that promised equality for all people.

6.   How was the fear of tissue culture portrayed?

    A.   It showed up in an episode of "Lights Out", a 1930s radio horror story of a fictional Dr. Alberts who'd created an immortal chicken heart in his lab. It grew out of control overtaking everything in this path.

7.   Where did Carrel die?

    A.   He died awaiting trial for collaborating with the Nazis.

8.   Why was the discovery of Henrietta's growing cells tarnished?

    A.   Because of Carrel, people believed tissue culture was the stuff of racism, creepy science fiction, Nazis, and snake oil. It wasn't something to be celebrated.

CHAPTER 8

"A Miserable Specimen"

1. What is "benevolent deception?"

    A. Benevolent deception was a common medical practice of doctors withholding information from their patients so as not to confuse or upset patients with frightening terms they might not understand.

2. Why didn't black patients question their care?

    A. It was understood that black people didn't question white people's professional judgment because since discrimination was widespread, patients were just glad to be getting treatment.

3. Why weren't more people aware of Henrietta's quick decline?

    A. "Her looks and body did not fade," said Sadie. "Only her eyes were tellin you that she wasn't gonna be alive no more."

4. Why did nurses label Henrietta's drawn blood, COLORED?

    A. This was done in case she needed transfusions later.

5. What evidence supports the sentence, "Her doctors tried in vain to ease her suffering?"

    A. She was treated with Demerol, morphine, Dromoran, and alcohol injections but nothing worked.

6.   What did microbiologist, Laure Aurelian, say George Gey whis-
     pered to Henrietta?

     A.   He said, "Your cells will make your immortal." He told Hen-
          rietta her cells would help save the lives of countless people,
          and she smiled.

CHAPTER 9

Turner Station

1. Rebecca felt like she was in a "Twilight Zone" episode. What did she mean by this?

    A. She ended up reading an old copy of a "Rolling Stone" article written by Michael Rogers where he seemed to be recreating the same moment she was living with regards to research to Henrietta Lacks.

2. How had Turner Station changed since Henrietta lived there?

    A. When Henrietta lived there she never had to lock her doors. Now there was a housing project surrounded by a 13,000 –foot-long brick-and-cement security wall in the field where Henrietta's children once played. Stores, nightclubs, cafes, and schools had closed, and drug dealers, gangs, and violence were on the rise.

3. Who was Courtney Speed?

    A. Courtney Speed owned a grocery store and had created a foundation devoted to building a Henrietta Lacks museum.

4. Why didn't Courtney tell Rebecca what she knew of Henrietta?

    A. She said she would tell Rebecca everything she knew when she had talked to the family.

5.   What videotape had Courtney given Rebecca before she turned and walked out of the door, locking it?

   A.   BBC documentary about Henrietta and the HeLa cells, called "The Way of All Flesh"

6.   What did viewing the video help Henrietta decide?

   A.   She needed to go to Clover and find Henrietta's cousins.

CHAPTER 10

The Other Side of the Tracks

1. The author says, "The other business looked like someone left for lunch decades earlier and never bothered coming back." What evidence supports this statement?

   A. boarded-up gas stations, RIP painted on fronts of buildings, cave in theater roof, walled lined with new Red Wing work boots stacked to the ceiling

2. What evidence proves "the dividing line between Lacks Town and the rest of Clover was stark?"

   A. One side had well-manicured rolling hills, acres and acres of wide-open property with horses, a small pond, a well-kept house set back from the road, a minivan, and a white picket fence. Directly across the street was a one-room shack about seven feet wide and twelve foot long; it was made of unpainted wood, with large gaps between the wallboards where vines and weeds grew.

3. What is meant by the statement, "if we could get all the pieces of her together, she'd weigh over eight hundred pounds now?"

   A. There were that many HeLa cells out there that they would weigh over eight hundred pounds.

4. What is meant that some things are man-made (voodoo)?

   A. Some said Henrietta's sickness and her cells were man-or-woman-made. Others say it was doctor-made.

5. Were the residents in Lacks Town superstitious? Explain your answer.

   A. Cootie believes there were spirits in Lacks Town causing disease. Examples are the headless hog and clanking chains.

6. What was Cootie's view of Henrietta's cancer?

   A. "Her cancer was no regular cancer, cause regular cancer don't keep on growing after a person die."

CHAPTER 11

"The Devil of Pain Itself"

1. How could Henrietta ensure she could continue to get transfusions?

    A. She had to make up the deficit with the blood bank to continue her transfusions.

2. How was this deficit satisfied?

    A. Henrietta's cousin Emmett gathered his brother and friends from Sparrow Point to give blood.

3. What memory will Emmett always remember about visiting Henrietta in the hospital?

    A. "Henrietta rose up out that bed wailin like she been possessed by the devil of pain itself.

4. Her chart stated at this time, "discontinue all medications and treatment except analgesics." What is an analgesic?

    A. An analgesic is a drug dispensed for relieving pain.

5. When did Henrietta die?

    A. Henrietta died at 12:15 a.m. on October 4, 1951.

CHAPTER 12

The Storm

1. Why did George Gey insist on an autopsy of Henrietta?

    A. Gey wanted samples from as many organs in her body as possible to see if they would grow like HeLa.

2. What was the difference in laws and ethics when dealing with a living person and one that had died?

    A. No law or code of ethics required doctors to ask permission before taking tissue from a living patient. The laws made it clear that performing an autopsy or removing tissue from the dead without permission was illegal.

3. How did doctors convince Day to perform an autopsy on Henrietta?

    A. Doctors said they wanted to run tests that might help his children someday.

4. What did the autopsy reveal?

    A. The cause of death was terminal uremia: blood poisoning from the buildup of toxins. Tumors were everywhere.

5.   Describe Henrietta's funeral.

    A.   As her casket was lowered into the ground in Clover the sky turned black, rain fell thick and fast, thunder rumbled, scream from babies, winds causing fires and ripped trees out of the ground, and whipping a log cabin onto one of her cousins, killing him instantly.

CHAPTER 13

The HeLa Factory

1. Why was the HeLa factory built?

   A. It was built to produce trillions of cells to help stop polio.

2. What is the relationship between HeLa, Jonas Salk, and NFIP?

   A. Jonas Salk developed a vaccine for polio in 1952. NFIP (National Foundation for Infantile Paralysis helped with the largest field trial ever to test this vaccine. HeLa was more susceptible to the virus than all other.

      Additional links: http://www.salk.edu/about/jonas_salk.html

      http://www.cdc.gov/polio/

3. Why was Tuskegee Institute chosen to conduct the research and development of polio vaccine?

   A. Tuckegee Institute was chosen because Charles Bynum, director of Negro Activities for the foundation, because it would provide hundreds of thousands of dollars in funding, many jobs, and training opportunities for young black scientists.

      Additional links: http://www.tuskegee.edu/about_us/history_and_ mission.aspx

4.   Explain the irony of the polio studies being conducted at the same time as the syphilis studies.

    A. Answers will vary.

5.   How were HeLa cells like normal cells?

    A.   Both kinds of cell produced proteins and communicated with one another, they divided and generated energy, they expressed genes and regulated them, and they were susceptible to infections.

6.   Why is HeLa a "workhorse"?

    A.   It was hardy, inexpensive, and it was everywhere.

7.   How did HeLa help virology?

    A.   HeLa was exposed to viruses such as herpes, measles, mumps, fowl pox, and equine encephalitis.

8.   What did scientists discover about freezing HeLa?

    A.   They could freeze HeLa without harming or changing the cells. Freezing allowed scientists to send cells around the world, store cells between uses, and suspend cells in various states of being.

9.   What happened to change standardization of tissue culture, "that at that point, was a bit of a mess?"

    A.   Tuskegee began mass-producing HeLa; 2) With the help of Harry Eagle culture medium could be made by the gallon and shipped ready to use; 3) Gey and others determined which glassware and stoppers were the least toxic to cells.

10.   Why were cellular clones important?

    A.   Scientists wanted to grow cellular clones—lines of cells descended from individual cells—so they could harness unique traits.

11. What laboratory accident proved to be a fortunate mistake?

    A. When a scientist accidentally mixed the wrong liquid with HeLa and a few other cells causing the chromosomes to swell and spread out, they discovered that normal human cells have forty-six chromosomes.

12. How did HeLa become big business?

    A. Answers will vary.

13. How did HeLa aid in women's health?

    A. HeLa was used in cosmetic and pharmaceutical companies instead of lab animals to test whether new products would cause cellular damage. They also tested the effects of steroids, chemotherapy drugs, hormones, vitamins, and environmental stress by infecting them with tuberculosis, salmonella, and the bacterium that causes vaginitis.

CHAPTER 14

Helen Lane

1. Once Gey had released HeLa as general scientific property, people started wondering about the woman behind the cells. Why, then, was the name Henrietta Lacks such a mystery?

    A. Answers will vary.

CHAPTER 15

"Too Young to Remember"

1. What was brought to Henrietta's funeral besides good wishes?

    A. A family member or friend brought tuberculosis and within a week Sonny, Deborah, and baby Joe tested positive.

2. Why didn't the children know what happened to their mother?

    A. Back then, the rule of the house was, "Do what adults say—otherwise you'll get hurt."

3. What happened to Henrietta's children once she died and Day needed help?

    A. Years of abuse occurred at the hands of Ethel. Describe the abuse.

4. What was the result of Ethel's abuse on Joe?

    A. After years of beatings, Joe stopped feeling pain: he felt only rage.

5. What was Deborah's problem during this time?

    A. Galen, Ethel's husband, was Deborah's biggest problem, and he found her wherever she went.

6.   Bobbett was a positive influence on Deborah. Explain

   A.   She intervened between Deborah and Ethel and Galen's abuse by saying that if either of them touched the Lacks children again, she'd kill them herself. She also made Deborah understand that cousins are not supposed to be having sex with each other. Deborah and her sibling had hearing problems because Henrietta and Day were first cousins. She insisted Deborah go to school.

CHAPTER 16

"Spending Eternity in the Same Place"

1. Cootie, Henrietta's cousin, said, "It sound strange, but her cell done lived longer than her memory." What is the inference?

   A. People did not talk to each other; not about Henrietta, not about her cancer.

2. Cliff, a cousin a Henrietta's, gave the author valuable background for her research. Summarize that background.

   A. Answers will vary.

3. How did the Lacks family cemetery differentiate between members who had money and the ones who did not?

   A. The wealthy had homemade tombstones made of concrete or store-bought out of marble. Those who were poor had graves marked with index-card-sized metal plates or unmarked. There were so many people buried in the family cemetery that they were piling graves on top of each other.

4. According to Cliff what was beautiful about the slave-owning white Lackses being buried under their black kin?

   A. "They spending eternity in the same place. They must've worked out their problems by now!"

5. Summarize the slave, slave owner relationship that began the Lacks family line.

    A. Various answers.

6. What was meant by "Lillian converted to Puerto Rican?"

    A. Henrietta's youngest sister, Lillian, married a Puerto Rican and because her skin was light, she could pass so she disowned her blackness because she didn't want to be black no more.

CHAPTER 17

Illegal, Immoral, and Deplorable

1. What was Chester Southam's concern, as a virologist, about the HeLa cells?

   A. Could the cells infect the scientists working with them.

2. How did Southam test for this concern?

   A. He injected unsuspecting patients with millions of HeLa cells.

3. Why wasn't testing with cancer patients conclusive?

   A. He needed to see how healthy patients would react to the injection of HeLa cells.

4. How did Southam gain these patients?

   A. He placed an ad for volunteers in the Ohio State Penitentiary newsletter.

5. Why aren't prisoners used today for testing?

   A. In fifteen years research on inmates would become heavily regulated because they would be considered a vulnerable population. But during this time (1950s) inmates were used for testing in many ways.

6. Why did the press hail these results a success?

   A. The inmates seemed to be fight off these cells so perhaps this could lead to a cancer vaccine.

7. Why did Southam withhold information from the patients he was testing?

   A. People have a natural phobia and ignorance that surrounds the word *cancer*.

8. Why did doctors find a problem with the arrangement Southam had with Emanuel Mandel from the Jewish Chronic Disease Hospital in Brooklyn?

   A. Three young Jewish doctors knew about the research done on Jewish prisoners and the Nuremberg Trials.

   Additional links: http://law2.umkc.edu/faculty/projects/ftrials/nuremberg/nuremberg.htm

9. How did the Nuremberg Code affect the Hippocratic oath?

   A. The Nuremberg Code governs all human experimentation worldwide. It states, "Voluntary consent of the human subjects is absolutely essential." The Hippocratic oath, written in the fourth century did not require this.

10. Why were regulations regarding human experimentation repeatedly shot down?

    A. These were voted down for fear of interfering with the progress of science.

11. What case caused *informed consent* to appear in court document?

    A. When Martin Salgo was placed under anesthesia for a routine procedure and awoke permanently paralyzed, the civil court ruled that there needed to be "full disclosure of facts necessary to an informed consent."

12. William Hyman, a lawyer, compared Southam's study to Nazi research by calling it *illegal, immoral, and deplorable.* Explain.

A. Answers will vary. Use as a high school debate issue.

13. What happened when NIH became involved with Southam's work?

A. NIH stated that all funded research on human subjects had to be approved by review boards (independent bodies made up of professionals and laypeople of diverse races, classes, and background to ensure of meeting ethics requirements.

14. How did science react to these new requirements?

A. Scientists said medical research was doomed, progress ceased.

Additional links: http://www.hhs.gov/ohrp/archive/documents/BeecherArticle.pdf

CHAPTER 18

"Strangest Hybrid"

1. How did HeLa behave in space?

    A. Noncancerous cells grew normally in orbit, but HeLa became more powerful, dividing faster with each trip.

2. How did Lewis Coriell explain all cancerous cells behaving the same?

    A. He felt that these cells behaved the same because viruses or bacterium had contaminated them.

3. The growing library of cells revealed what discoveries?

    A. Cigarettes caused lung cancer, X-rays and certain chemicals transformed normal cells into malignant ones; normal cells stopped growing and cancer cells didn't; cells helped screen 30,000 chemicals and plant extracts yielding effective chemotherapy drugs.

4. Discuss how many scientists became cavalier about their cultures.

    A. Answers vary.

5.   Robert Stevenson and the ATCC set up protective measures to ensure pure cell cultures. What were they?

    A.   Working under hoods with suction that pulled air and potential contaminants into a filtration system, establishing a central bank where all cultures would be tested, cataloged, and stored under maximum security.

6.   Describe the Fort Knox of pure, uncontaminated cell cultures at the ATCC.

    A.   Answers vary

        Additional links: http://www.atcc.org/Products/Cells%20 and%20Microorganisms/Cell%20Lines.aspx

7.   What is somatic cell fusion or "cell sex"?

    A.   Cells infected with certain viruses clumped together and fused, combining genetic material.

8.   What were contributions of Henry Harris and John Watkins?

    A.   By fusing HeLa cells with mouse cells and developing hybrids they could study what genes do and how they work, forming gene therapy.

9.   What were some results from this study?

    A.   Hybruids created the first monoclonal antibodies, helped study the role of immunity in organ transplantation.

10.   Why were some concerned about these discoveries?

    A.   "Scientists Create Monsters" was the concern.

CHAPTER 19

"The Most Critical Time on this Earth Is Now"

1. Describe Crazy Joe and how he ended up in prison.

   A. Answers will vary.

2. Describe Deborah and her life with Cheetah.

   A. Answers will vary.

CHAPTER 20
The HeLa Bomb

1. Stanley Gartler discovered a technical problem with cell cultures. What was it?

    A. Eighteen unrelated cell cultures had one thing in common. They all had a rare genetic marker called G6PD-A that was exclusively found in black Americans.

2. What did this prove?

    A. HeLa contamination.

3. How powerful were HeLa cells?

    A. They could float through air on dust particles, travel from one culture to another on unwashed hands or used pipettes, ride on researchers coats and shoes, or through ventilation systems.

4. What precautions did Stevenson and like-minded scientists take?

    A. They began working to develop genetic tests that could specifically identify HeLa cells in culture.

CHAPTER 21

Night Doctors

1. What had Lawrence heard about the importance of his mother's cells?

    A. He heard that his mother's cells were a miracle. That by 2050 babies will be injected with serum made from HeLa so that they can live to be 800 years old. They're going to get rid of disease, help grow a cornea for transplanting.

2. How did Sonny and Day feel about doctors?

    A. Although both were suffering from several maladies, they had a basic fear of doctors. They didn't want doctors cutting on them like they did Henrietta.

3. How did the doctors appeal to Day about giving Henrietta an autopsy?

    A. They said they wanted to do this to "help my children, my grandchildren."

4. What are "night doctors?"

    A. Since the 1800s oral history tells how black people were kidnapped for research. Some tales told by white plantation owners to discourage slaves from meeting or escaping gave rise to the white hooded cloaks of the KKK.

5.   What procedures did doctors use on slaves?

    A.   Doctors tested drugs on slaves and operated on them. An underground shipping industry kept schools in black bodies arriving in turpentine-filled barrels.

5.   Why was John Hopkins built?

    A.   It was built for the benefit of Baltimore's poor.

6.   Why is the history of Hopkins muddied?

    A.   In 1969, a Hopkins researcher used blood samples from neighborhood children to test for a genetic predisposition to criminal behavior. Also thirty years later women claimed researchers knowingly exposed their children to lead.

7.   What was the irony expressed by Lawrence?

    A.   "She's (our mother) the most important person in the world and her family living in poverty."

8.   What really upset the Lackes?

    A.   Dr. Gey never told the family anything—they didn't know anything about those cells.

CHAPTER 22

"The Fame She So Richly Deserves"

1.   What is GeGe?

   A.   This was the result of a procedure done on George Gey discovering he had pancreatic cancer. He wanted his cells to be immortal like Henrietta's.

2.   While writing a tribute of Gey's career, Howard Jones searched Henrietta's records and discovered a misdiagnosis. What was it?

   A.   The original doctor had "misinterpreted" or "mislabeled" Henrietta's cancer, which would explain why the cancer spread throughout her body faster than expected.

3.   Henrietta's photo is called ubiquitous. This means?

   A.   Ubiquitous means everywhere at the same time. Constantly.

4.   What is the National Cancer Act?

   A.   Richard Nixon signed into law $1.5 billion for cancer research by both American and Russian scientists.

5.   Explain the *scarlet H*.

   A.   Walter Nelson-Rees was hired to help stop the contamination problem by issuing "HeLa Hit Lists."

CHAPTER 23

"It's Alive"

1. What is the Human Genome Project?

   Additional Links: http://www.genome.gov/12011238

2. What was the answer to the contamination problem?

   A. The problem could be solved with finding genetic markers specific to Henrietta. This could only be accomplished with DNA samples from her immediate family.

3. Who is Victor McKusick?

   A. He was a geneticist who found the first genetics department at Hopkins, cataloging hundreds of genes into a database, Mendelian Inheritance in Man.

4. Why was language a problem between Hsu and Day?

   A. Hsu's accent was strong and so was Day's so when he didn't understand something a doctor said, he nodded and said yes.

5. McKusick began his research on the Lacks family at a time of great flux. What does this mean?

   A. HEW was investigating unethical studies at this time with "widespread confusion about how to assess risk."

6. Deborah was a hard worker. Explain.

   A. Answers will vary.

7. Explain the new risk from the new era of genetic research.

   A. Once someone uncovered your genetic information would your privacy be violated?

CHAPTER 24

"Least They Can Do"

1. How did Michael Rogers help inform the Lacks about the HeLa contamination problem?

    A. A report from the Rolling Stone said researchers around the world were purchasing small glass vials for about $25 to use in cell lines.

2. Gey profited from the sale of HeLa and he became wealthy. True or False. Explain.

    A. Answers will vary but should include that Gey wasn't interested in science for profit.

3. Have others profited from HeLa sales?

    A. Invitrogen sells HeLa products costing $100—$10,000 per vial.

4. Why was Deborah terrified by HeLa?

    A. She imagined people-plants when she found out that HeLa had been crossed with tobacco plants. She felt her mother's eternal suffering when she learned HeLa was being used to study AIDS and Ebola.

    Additional Links: https://docs.google.com/file/d/0B7i3t9b 0_9jRYjMxNTg2ZDItNzVmMy00YjUzLWJhYmMtNW FlMTMwOTE3N2Rh/edit?hl=en_US&pli=1

5. Why was the timely release of Mike Roger's article explosive?

    A. Several events occurred at the same time: Tuskegee study, racist health-care systems declared by the Pink Panthers, and Henrietta's racial story.

6. Why would no scientist today publish a name with his genetic information?

    A. Because we know today information from DNA can include risks for developing certain diseases.

7. What is HIPAA?

    A. It's the Health Insurance Portability and Accountability Act that protects personal medical information. Violations could result in fines and jail time.

8. How was John Moore's fight different yet similar to that of the Lackses family?

    A. He had knowledge on his side and he had the means to hire a lawyer.

CHAPTER 25

"Who Told You You Could Sell My Spleen?"

1. What was John Moore's illness?

    A. While working on the Alaskan Pipeline, Moor developed symptoms that led to a diagnosis of hairy-cell leukemia.

2. How did Moore handle his consent form?

    A. Even after writing "do not" consent form, Dr. Golde filed a patent on John Moore's cells. To date the market value of Mo cells is abut $3billion.

3. Who is Ananda Mohan Chakrabarty?

    A. He created a bacterium genetically engineered to consume oil and help clean up spills. His patent was denied on the grounds that no living organism could be considered an invention. This was overturned when discovered his bacterium were not naturally occurring.

4. How did Ted Slavin deal with his antibodies?

    A. Ted Slavin was born a hemophiliac and told by his doctor that he was producing something extremely valuable. He began dealing directly with the labs to supply blood for hepatitis B research.

5.   What was the definitive statement on the issue of who owns cells and tissues?

   A.   "When tissues are removed from your body, with or without your consent, any claim you might have had to owning them vanishes."

CHAPTER 26
Breach of Privacy

1.   What was the "big payday" for the Lacks family?

   A.   Day and others settled with a boiler manufacturer over damages done to lungs from asbestos exposure at Bethlehem Steel. Day shared his $12,000 with his children.

2.   How did Deborah learn about how Henrietta suffered while hospitalized in the 50s?

   A.   She learned for the first time about the excruciating pain, fever, and vomiting; poisons building in her blood. This was also the first time she would learn about the results of the autopsy: the grey and white tumor globules. Strings of "pearls" ran over the surface of the organs.

CHAPTER 27

The Secret of Immortality

1. What did Harald zur Hausen discover through his research in 1984?

    A. He discovered a new strain of STD called Human Papilloma Virus 18. HeLa cells tested positive for HPV-18 causing a virulent reaction in Henrietta's cervix.

2. What other landmark moment occurred in the eighties?

    A. HeLa was used in HIV research.

3. What was meant by the statement, "HeLa cells have become a separate species.?"

    A. By the eighties HeLa had given rise to many tons of other cells but slightly different from the original. He said HeLa cells are evolving separately from humans, and having a separate evolution is really what a species is all about.

4. Why don't scientists like to associate HeLa with Henrietta as a person?

    A. It's easier to do science when you disassociate your materials from the people they came from. Henrietta's DNA fingerprint would match the DNA in HeLa cells.

5.   What is the Hayflick Limit?

    A.   The Hayflick Limit is the finite number of times a normal human cell can divide.

6.   What cells are immortal?

    A.   Only cells that had been transformed by a virus or a genetic mutation had the potential to become immortal.

7.   What is a telomere?

    A.   Each chromosome has a string of DNA at its end that shortens a bit after each cell division.

8.   Explain telomerase.

    A.   Telomerase is an enzyme that rebuilds telomeres, which explain the immortality of HeLa.

CHAPTER 28

After London

1. Why was 1996-1999 referred to as after London?

    A. BBC producer Adam Curtis produced documentary about Henrietta.

2. Who was Roland Patillo?

    A. He was the scientist who put the author, Rebecca Skloot, in touch with Deborah.

3. The BBC created more questions for Deborah. What did she decide to do?

    A. She requested a copy of Henrietta's hospital records from Hopkins along with a copy of her sister's records.

4. Why did Deborah think people were hiding things from her?

    A. Answers will vary.

CHAPTER 29
A Village of Henriettas

1. What were the conditions for Deborah to tell her story?

   A. First, get her mother's name right. Second tell everyone she had five kids not four.

2. What if FISH?

   A. Fluorescence in situ hybridization is a multi-colored dye for painting chromosomes under an ultraviolet light.

3. "Deborah's was a world without silence." Explain.

   A. Answers will vary.

4. "Deborah was full of oddly charming quirks." Explain.

   A. Answers will vary.

CHAPTER 30
Zakariyya

1. Zakariyya is an important contact for the author. Describe him.

    A. Answers will vary.

CHAPTER 31

HeLa, Goddess of Death

1. Why was Deborah told not to talk to white people about the story?

   A. Everyone was screaming racism, because, in their minds, it was a white woman who killed a black woman.

2. Why wouldn't Deborah let Rebecca see her mother's medical records?

   A. She was afraid that Rebecca was trying to steal them, and she needed someone she could trust.

3. What had Rebecca promised to do when and if her book was published?

   A. She promised to set up a scholarship fund for descendants of Henrietta Lacks.

4. Why was Deborah happy about this?

   A. Deborah believed, "Education is everything."

5. Trust in Rebecca didn't come easily. Explain.

   A. Answers will vary.

6.   Deborah and Rebecca's relationship was symbiotic. Explain.

      A.   Answers will vary.

7.   How could potential research on *Henrietta* or *lacks* or Hela be confusing?

      A.   HeLa is native name for the country of Sri Lanka; the name of an old German tractor company; the name of a shih-tzu dog; a seaside port in Poland; an advertising firm in Switzerland; the name of a Danish for socializing; a Marvel comic book character.

8.   When did Deborah begin taking on a bigger role in Rebecca's research?

      A.   When Deborah became more comfortable with the Internet, she made lists of questions and printed out articles about research.

9.   What was one form of recognition in Henrietta's honor?

      A.   Franklin Salisbury Jr., president of the National Foundation for Cancer Research wanted Deborah to speak at the 2001 conference and receive a plaque in Henrietta's honor.

CHAPTER 32

"All That's My Mother"

1. What was the purpose of Deborah and Rebecca visiting Christoph Lengauer's lab?

    A. Deborah wanted to see her mother's cells.

2. What did Lengauer mean when he said, "Seems like a bit of poetic justice, doesn't it?"

    A. HeLa contamination cost millions of dollars in damages while the industry kept secrets from the family.

3. How did Lengauer explain to Deborah the differences between a cell and DNA?

    A. He explained that DNA is inside the nucleus of a cell. Forty-six pieces of DNA in every cell make up chromosomes. He explained how Henrietta's cancer came from a DNA mistake; in Henrietta's case a HPV genital wart virus. He explained that this is not passed down to Henrietta's children.

4. How did Deborah and Zakariyya react when they saw their mother's cells divide?

    A. They were in a trance-like state because it was the closest they had come to seeing their mother alive since they were babies.

5.   Why was Deborah stunned by Dr. Lengauer's comment, "Yeah, Hopkins pretty much screwed up, I think."

   A.   She could not believe a scientist would say this.

6.   According to Lengauer, cells should be treated like oil. What did he mean?

   A.   When you find oil on your property, the owner gets part of the money; therefore, Henrietta's children should get a part of the profits from HeLa.

7.   Deborah said, "Girl, you just witnessed a miracle." What is she referring to?

   A.   Dr. Lengauer gave Deborah his cell phone number; she knew he cared.

CHAPTER 33

The Hospital for the Negro Insane

1. Crownsville did not look like what they expected. Explain

    A. Answers will vary.

2. What happened to the hospital records?

    A. Because of an asbestos problem, most records were carted away and buried.

3. Why did Deborah and Rebecca stare speechless at Elsie's photo?

    A. They witnessed a disturbing sight: frizzy matted hair, bulging eyes bruised and swollen shut, misshapen face with nostrils inflamed and ringed with mucus, swollen lips, She seems to be screaming and head turned into an unnatural twist held by white hands.

4. What did the article, "Overcrowded Hospital "Loses" Curable Patients" reveal? Describe the "Fearsome black wards?"

    A. Answers will vary.

5. What are pneumoencephalographic and x-ray studies?

    A   This was a technique developed to take pictures of the brain, floating in a sea of fluid. This is done by drilling into the skulls of research subjects, draining the fluid surrounding the brain, and then pumping air or helium into the skull. The side effects are crippling headaches, dizziness, seizures, vomiting.

6.   Why was Deborah distressed over The Washington Post article saying, "The worst thing you can do to a sick person is close the door and forget about him?"

    A.   Deborah did not know Elsie was there or she would have gotten her out.

        Additional Links: http://crownsvilleandtheinsanehospital. blogspot.com

CHAPTER 34

The Medical Records

1. What information was revealed when Rebecca was finally given access to Henrietta's medical records?

    A. While pregnant with Deborah, Henrietta was identified as Rh+; apparently was feeling fine on February 6, 1951 when she was first seen at Hopkins for her cervical cancer; Elsie was diagnosed with idiocy.

2. What misunderstanding occurred when Rebecca smiled at Deborah?

    A. Deborah thought Rebecca was lying to her.

3. Why didn't Deborah think Rebecca human?

    A. She didn't think Deborah human because she never saw her angry or heard her cuss.

CHAPTER 35

Soul Cleansing

1. Rebecca Skloot spent hours talking to Gary. Why

    A. After talking to Gary, Rebecca understood Deborah and that she had been through more than anyone else in the family.

2. How did Deborah respond when Gary told her, "Do something to relax yourself?"

    A. She said, "I worry all the time."

3. What does WWJD stand for?

    A. It stands for, "What Jesus Would Do."

4. Gary had healing powers. Explain.

    A. Using the Lord, Gary eased Deborah's burdens.

5. Rebecca states, "That wasn't supposed to happen." This refers to?

    A. Gary was transferring the burden of the cells from Deborah to Rebecca.

CHAPTER 36

Heavenly Bodies

1. Gary had an impact on Rebecca. Explain.

    A. For the first time in her life, Rebecca found herself humming a hymn. She also read from the Bible for the first time in her life.

2. Gary whispered, "Henrietta was chosen." What did Gary mean by this statement?

    A. He quoted from the scripture, "There are heavenly bodies and earthly bodies, the beauty that belongs to heavenly bodies is different from the beauty that belongs to earthy bodies."

        Also, "This is how it will be when the dead are raised, it will be immortal. There is, of course, a physical body, so there has to be a spiritual body."

3. How was the spiritual explanation of Henrietta's immortality different from the scientific explanation?

    A. Answers will vary but could include, "Jesus told his followers, 'I gave them eternal life, and they shall never die.'

CHAPTER 37

"Nothing to Be Scared About"

1. Deborah was suffering from serious health problems. What were the symptoms?

   A. She had symptoms of stroke and heart attack: confusion, panic, incoherent speech, redness and swelling.

2. How did Rebecca interact with Deborah because of Deborah's health?

   A. Rebeccca only told Deborah the "good" stories involved in her research.

3. Why did Deborah want to go back to school?

   A. She felt if he understood science, the stories about her mother and sister wouldn't scare her so much.

4. Why was the conference honoring Henrietta canceled?

   A. September 11, 2001 happened and the Ronald Reagan Building where the conference reception was to be held was being evacuated.

5.   "Boy, you did your grandmother a favor." This is referring to
      _____?

      A.   Davon, Deborah's grandson, rushed her to the fire station
            when he discovered she was suffering from a stroke. He
            saved her life.

6.   Why did Deborah's stroke ease tension in the family?

      A.   Her family members checked in on her regularly.

7.   What unexpected event occurred at Jabrea's baptism?

      A.   Pullman asked Rebecca to speak to everyone about what she
            was doing with his wife and them cells.

CHAPTER 38

The Long Road to Clover

1. Things always change. What change occurred on January 18, 2009 while Rebecca was driving to Clover?

   A.   Clover was gone.

2. Deborah's two favorite movies were *Roots* and *Spirit*, when watched together showed similarities to each other. What were they?

   A.   Spirit fought for his freedom just as Kunta Kinte did in Roots.

3. How does having a lock of her mother's hair help Deborah?

   A.   She said when she thinks about this hair, she is less lonely. She would like a mother to go to, to laugh, cry, or hug.

AFTERWORD

Additional Links:

Common Rule

http://www.hhs.gov/ohrp/humansubjects/commonrule/

Declaration of Helsinki
https://www.google.com/search?client=safari&rls=en&q=declara-
tion+of+helsinki&ie=UTF-8&oe=UTF-8

Belmont Report
http://www.hhs.gov/ohrp/humansubjects/guidance/belmont.html

Native American Havasupai Tribe
http://genetics.ncai.org/case-study/havasupai-Tribe.cfm

HIPPA
http://www.hhs.gov/ocr/privacy/index.html

Center for Biomedical Ethics and Society at Vanderbilt University

http://medicineandpublichealth.vanderbilt.edu/center.php?userid=147
886474&home=1

Consent diminishes the value of tissue.

http://www.nytimes.com/2006/04/16/magazine/16tissue.html?page-
wanted=all&_r=0

Myriad Genetics

WRITING WORKSHOP

THE ARGUMENT ESSAY

OVERVIEW	IMPORTANT ELEMENTS	TOPIC SELECTION
In preparing our students for college it is important to know that the argument essay may be one of the most common writing assignment they may encounter.	**Perform effective and thorough research** before committing to a topic to ensure enough credible resources for support. **Effective thesis statement** is important in any essay but especially important for the argument essay because the writer needs to identify the argument and why the argument is important. This cannot be confusing to the reader. **Necessary background information on the topic** supplies the needed details to support the thesis statement Because the argument essay involves multiple reasons and evidence to support overall thesis statement the writer should **focus on organization and transitions.** **Incorporate logos, pathos, and ethos** throughout the essay. Although logos (logic) should be the primary focus, pathos (emotion) can also be used for the argument essay. Ethos (credibility) is addressed by addressing counter arguments and using credible sources	**Current, debatable, researchable, and manageable** topics are best to use for the argument essay because they can be argued logically. A **current** topic is one that has not been over-debated and is still being decided. Avoid topics such as abortion, the death penalty, the legalization of marijuana. A **debatable** topic is controversial with differing viewpoints. Writing about domestic violence is not debatable since no one would disagree with this thesis. But debating whether common punishments for domestic violence are effective and a deterrent. A **researchable topic** can be supported with a variety of credible and current sources. A **manageable topic** is one that has been narrowed enough to meet the page requirement of the essay. Begin with a basic broad subject and then narrow it down to a subtopic.

CAUSE EFFECT ESSAY

OVERVIEW	TIPS
These essays are not to be about both causes and effects, but a focus on either cause or effect	**Introduction**—let your audience know what you are going write about. **Keep a narrow topical focus** and don't try to answer all causes or effects. Three or four is a good number to concentrate on. **Support all causes or effects with supporting details.** **Decide on the order in which to present information.** **Conclusion**—restate thesis or generalize your essay

COMPARE CONTRAST ESSAY

OVERVIEW	TIPS
These essays are huge in academic writing. They will follow a specific question and are fairly easy to complete. It is important to remember the structure and keep it consistent.	**Introduction**—like a five-paragraph essay, use a quotation, anecdote, generalization and then lead into the thesis statement. **Topic 1**—cover only the first topic of the comparison and contrast. Do not mention topic 2 in the first part. **Topic 2**—cover the second of the two topics. Do not discuss topic 1 here. **Topics 1 & 2 together**—Now analyze both topics together in one or multiple paragraphs. **Conclusions**—should be a generalization of the thesis as in introduction. Reaffirm your thesis. You complete knowledge of the subject should be apparent.

THE EVALUATION ESSAY

OVERVIEW	IMPORTANT ELEMENTS	TOPIC SELECTION
The purpose of an evaluation essay is to demonstrate the overall quality (or lack thereof) of a particular product, business, place, service, or program. While opinions are interjected naturally in this essay, if done properly the evaluation should seem reasoned and unbiased.	An overall **thesis** should be offered. Having clear **criteria** (ideal for the product/place/service/etc.) is what keeps an evaluation from feeling less like an opinion. The **judgment** is the establishment of whether or not the criterion is met. In other words, the judgment is what actually is. The **evidence** is the details offered to support the judgment Each body paragraph of an evaluation should **focus on one specific criterion,** which should be fully explained, followed by the judgment and a variety of evidence offered as support. Consequently all evaluations should contain several **different** criteria, judgments, and evidence	Focus on **specific business, service, product, or policy.** Write about a topic that you **have knowledge about** to make it easier to establish the appropriate criteria, judgments, and evidence.

THE INVESTIGATIVE ESSAY

OVERVIEW	IMPORTANT ELEMENTS	TOPIC SELECTION
Although similar to an argumentative essay, an investigative essay is often a precursor to an argument. The investigative essay allows for opinions and personal experiences, a difference from the argument essay.	In order to demonstrate a thorough knowledge of the subject, the writer **researches, researches, researches.** Writer must expertly interpret **research** and **articulate the various viewpoints** of the issue. The best investigative essays begin with a **legitimate question** to research, one that the writer is exploring.	**Current, debatable, researchable, and manageable** topics are best to use for the argument essay because they can be argued logically. A **current** topic is one that has not been over-debated and is still being decided. Avoid topics such as abortion, the death penalty, the legalization of marijuana. A **debatable** topic is controversial with differing viewpoints. Writing about domestic violence is not debatable since no one would disagree with this thesis. But debating whether common punishments for domestic violence are effective and a deterrent. A **researchable topic** can be supported with a variety of credible and current sources. A **manageable topic** is one that has been narrowed enough to meet the page requirement of the essay. Begin with a basic broad subject and then narrow it down to a subtopic.

PERSONAL ESSAY

OVERVIEW	TIPS
Often incorporating a variety of writing styles, the personal essay asks the writer to write about an important person, event, or time period in his/her life. The goal is to narrate this event in a way that uses both narrative and descriptive writing, which are two of the main models in writing.	**Focus on detail**—show, not tell using strong verbs, not overusing adjectives. **Use sensory detail**—bring the reader farther by using a variety of senses: sound, smell, touch, taste, in addition to sight. **Connect the event/person/place to a larger idea**—don't lose focus on the main idea: how the event changed you. It's the importance of the event that counts. **Be careful with verb tense**—when in doubt, stick with **past** tense for the actual event and **present** tense to discuss the change.

RESPONDING TO AN ESSAY

OVERVIEW	APPROACHES
Often following a literature summary, the writer responds to the piece subjectively using well -supported opinions and personal experiences. The thesis is the overall opinion of the essay you are responding to. Always be specific and always have support.	Agree or disagree with **the author's main point or thesis.** Agree or disagree with **the extent to which the thesis is made.** Agree or disagree with **specific points that are made that relate to the thesis.** Agree or disagree with **specific evidence that is offered in support of the thesis** Agree or disagree with **the relevancy of the overall topic.**

SUMMARIZING

OVERVIEW	TIPS
Although the shortest piece of writing in a high school course, it is not easy. A good summary accurately describes the main point and important details of the piece. In order to be accurate and concise the writer must be thoroughly familiar with the original work. If too long, a summary may be paraphrasing the original work, bit if too short, important details may be left out. Think one quarter to one third of the total length of the original article.	Read and **reread** essay as many times as necessary to gain a full understanding of it. No **first person statements** allowed. Opinions are not needed here. **Always name the author and article title** in the introductory paragraph, usually in the first or second sentence. From then on refer to author by **last name.** **Always use present tense** to discuss the essay and facts from the essay. Use **direct quotes or paraphrase** examples to support your claims. When talking about an essay or article, **always capitalize the title and place it in quotation marks.** Do not use italics.

CPSIA information can be obtained at www.ICGtesting.com
Printed in the USA
LVOW05s0454230514

387054LV00002B/247/P

9 781457 524141